608

The Best Of
TRY THIS ONE

Ideas for
youth groups

The Best Of
TRY THIS ONE

Edited by Thom Schultz

Illustrations by Rand Kruback and Alan Wilkes

Ideas for youth groups

Group
Books

P.O. Box 481
Loveland, Colorado 80539

Selected from the regular feature "Try This One" in GROUP,
the youth ministry magazine.

The Best Of
TRY THIS ONE

Copyright © 1977 and 1981 by Thom Schultz
Publications, Inc.

Sixth Printing

ISBN 0936-664-01-0

Table of Contents

Introduction

Some of the ideas to follow are serious. Some are funny. Some are very meaningful. Some are just crazy.

Do such a varied lot of ideas belong in a Christian group? I believe they do. Young people themselves are at various times serious, funny, meaningful and crazy. And if a group is to minister to the whole person, we must recognize the various sides that make up the whole person.

The following ideas were contributed to GROUP Magazine by Christian youth group members and leaders from all over the country. These ideas work. They're some of the best ideas in use today.

Use these ideas, modify them, enlarge upon them—and send us your ideas.

—Thom Schultz

Fun 'n Games

GARGLE CHAMP

You probably have always wondered who can gargle the longest in your group. Well, here's a great opportunity to discover the Champion Gargler.

Have two to six people volunteer to stand in front of the group. Each should take a mouth full of water—then gargle with gusto. No swallowing is allowed. You may pause to take one breath every few seconds. Water spilled on the floor from a laughing gargler disqualifies same gargler.

The gargler who gargles the longest wins. You might award a bottle of Scope. This is a gross game—but it's fun to watch!

SCRAMBLED EGGS

Blindfold two or four people (the more squeamish they are, the better). Ask them to remove their shoes, but keep their socks on.

Before they are blindfolded, show them a dozen eggs being placed on the floor. Now they will memorize where the eggs are, thinking that the object is to walk through without stepping on an egg.

But, the fun thing is that the eggs are taken away while the people are blindfolded. Crackers (three high) and water are placed on the walk. One by one, the blindfolded people walk through. When they think they've stepped on an egg, they really dance!

LEVITATION

Here's a great gag to spark up a meeting.

Find a strong board measuring about 12" x 36". Blindfold your "victim" and have him stand on the board, facing one of the ends. Tell him that two kids will stand beside him. He is to hold onto their shoulders to help him keep his balance.

Now, two other kids each grab one end of the board and lift it off the floor.

Then, as the board is held just a few inches off the floor, the two kids the "victim" is grabbing begin to slowly bend their knees, sinking gradually to the floor.

Your blindfolded "victim" will believe he is being lifted above everyone's heads as his helpers drop out of reach. Watch him weave, scream, panic and "fall" the frightening six inches to the floor below.

If you plan to try this gag on a number of "victims," make sure everyone who is not wise to the gag is kept out of eyeshot of the "levitation."

QUICK CHANGE ARTISTS

Pair off into partners facing each other. Each player is to observe his partner's appearance. Then the players turn around back to back and make two or more changes in their dress, hair, accessories, etc. When they face each other again, each partner must identify the changes made by his partner. This game can be repeated several times by changing partners and increasing the number of changes made.

TIMED PERSUASION

For this one, you'll need a room with a telephone, a tape recorder, and an inexpensive telephone recorder microphone. These little gadgets, available at electronics and discount stores, have a small suction cup on one end that attaches to the receiver of any phone.

Before your meeting, select three or four volunteers. Then, tell them that they will call a friend and convince him of something in the shortest amount of time. The conversation on the phone is to be recorded.

Then, assign each volunteer a situation. Example: Call a friend and convince him to go out with your cousin who's visiting from out of town. You must tell your friend that your cousin is a bit corpulent (overweight) and isn't too good-looking, but has a nice personality. Another example: Call a friend and convince him to call one of your teachers from school and ask the teacher what kind of mouthwash he/she uses.

When all your volunteers have recorded their conversations, they can return to the meeting room with the recordings. Then, the entire group will doubtless double over with laughter listening to these efforts in persuasion. A prize should go to the person who convinced his friend in the least amount of time. And you might also give a judge's award to the funniest conversation.

RHINOCEROS AND HIPPOPOTAMUS

Here's a good game to do at camp or just at a meeting. It turns from simplicity to confusion to hilarity.

Everyone sits in a circle. One person passes an object, like a spoon, to the person on his left. The passer says, "This is a rhinoceros." The passee says, "A what?" The passer repeats, "A rhinoceros." The spoon is then passed to the next person, with the new passer saying, "This is a rhinoceros." The new passee asks, "A what?" And the passer then asks the original passer, "A what?" The original answers, and the response is passed on around to the new passee. This progresses, with the question, "A what?" always returning all the way back to the original passer.

At the same time the spoon is passed to the left, the original passer also passes a spatula to the person on his right. He says to the passee, "This is a hippopotamus." The passee asks, "A what?" And so on, just like the spoon.

After both objects (they need not be a spoon and spatula) get started around the circle, soon the two "a whats" will collide, confusion will set in, and laughter usually destroys the rest of the game.

HUMAN TIC-TAC-TOE

The ancient game of tic-tac-toe can take on new excitement in your group by making it life-size.

Set up nine chairs in three rows—just like the sections on a tic-tac-toe diagram. Then divide your group into two teams. Each team takes its turn by sending one person to sit in a selected chair. The first team to get three-in-a-row wins.

Since you're not using Xs and Os, everybody really has to concentrate on who is on which team.

To make it a bit more exciting, establish a time limit that each team member has to select a seat. Give each person, say, five seconds after the last person sat down to reach the chosen chair.

CARD TEST

Attention grabber for your next meeting: On a postcard make a triangle in one corner, then write the following on the card: "Hold this triangle to your face and blow on it. If it turns green, call your physician. If it turns brown, see your dentist. If it turns purple, see your psychiatrist. If it turns black, call your lawyer and make a will. If it remains the same color, you are in good health and there is no reason on earth why you should not be in attendance at our next meeting." Mail to each member.

CHUCKLE CHAIN

The average person feels somewhat awkward and inhibited when introduced into a new group. With time these feelings usually fade as people warm up to each other, but that first introduction is always difficult.

The following activity can help to loosen up these tight moments and develop a sense of confidence and trust between group members, both of which can help make a person feel more comfortable in a new group.

Chuckle Chain can also be used to warm up or "break the ice" at a party. Developing trust and releasing undesired tensions can help to make a party or group activity a more "alive" and rewarding experience.

Chuckle Chain takes place as follows:

A) Depending on the size of the group, prepare a large floor-space or ground area, free from any obstacles or debris.

B) The first group member, preferably someone who knows how Chuckle Chain works, lies down on his/her back at one corner of the open space.

C) A second group member then lies down at a right angle to the first, with his/her head lying on the first member's stomach, and with legs pointed toward the largest area of open space.

A. WILKES

D) The remaining members, then, doing as the second member did, lie down on their backs one by one with heads on each others' stomachs, until the entire group is chained together in this way.

E) Once everyone is in position, the first member begins the Chuckle Chain with one "ha" or chuckle, since he/she is the first member of the chain.

F) The second member then chuckles twice, and the third chuckles three times, and the fourth four, and so on until the end of the chain is reached.

Note: The motion of the stomach of the person chuckling is more than likely going to make the person whose head is resting on that member's stomach begin to chuckle also, which in turn will jostle the next person's head, and the chuckles of the first member will involuntarily pass down the chain in this way. The objective of the exercise (though not to be stressed too severely) is to get through the entire chain without breaking up completely, or without losing count.

G) If the group is particularly small, or if the first member feels that everyone has not had enough chuckles to loosen them up, he/she might decide to repeat the chain, or perhaps try any one of an endless number of variations, such as: accumulating larger and larger numbers of chuckles using only odd or even numbers of chuckles, chuckling to a beat, etc.

SPARKING

It may not be necessary to get all nervous and bothered the next time someone asks you if he may "turn you on," "light your fire," "charge you up," etc. What he has in mind might be an offer to go "sparking" with him. By the way—if that's what he has in mind, take him up on it.

Here are some ground rules for "sparking" in your group:

1) "Sparking" must always be done with a member of the opposite sex.

2) No boyfriend-girlfriend couples (potentially too dangerous for that).

3) Wear loose fitting clothes that stretch and are easily cleaned.

4) Be prepared to look like a wreck after the "sparking" session.

5) There must never be any observers, only partici-pants. (After one becomes more adept at "sparking," "group sparking" might be enjoyed.)

6) Find an absolutely pitch dark place to "spark."

7) And finally, to make the event really pleasant, have several wintergreen Lifesavers for each participant. (This is to ensure a fresh breath for "sparking"—after all, who would want to "spark" with someone who has a "dragon in his mouth"?)

Really play it up. Find someone who has never "sparked." Try to convince her that you want to introduce her to the event of all times. Suggest that this might be an experience she will cherish for life.

After a long prelude to what will be expected, take the person and several wintergreen Lifesavers to a dark place. Each person takes a Lifesaver, faces the other person, puts the Lifesaver in the back of his mouth and bites down with mouth open. Lots of little blue and green sparks will appear. (We don't know why, but it just does.)

After "sparking," each person should mess up his hair and clothes (you could even smear a little lipstick on each other). Do anything that might free non-participants to suspect that "sparking" is even more of a "good time" than it is.

The only general response from new "sparkers" is, "Is that all there is to it?" Yes, that's all there is.

DRIP-DROP A SPONSOR

Pick two persons (usually the youth leader and spouse) and have them lie on the floor with a Coke bottle balanced on their foreheads. In the meantime, the group splits up into two teams. Each team has a tablespoon and a bowl of water.

The object? While standing straight up, the team members must try to hit the Coke bottle with a spoonful of water. The team that reaches an inch mark on the bottle wins.

The results are outrageous! But no spirits are dampened—only people!

MY PROBLEM

Divide into two teams. Each team sits in rows facing each other. Give each person a paper and pencil. Ask those on one side to write down some great predicament they imagine themselves in.

Those on the other side, without communicating with the first team, should write down a solution to some predicament.

After everyone has written down a predicament or a solution, the first person in one line states his predicament. Then the person opposite him says the solution he had written down. This continues down until everyone has had a turn. The results are pretty amusing.

SCRIPTURE MIXER

If you're planning a big get-together with many youth groups, here's an idea.

Hand out slips of paper with vital parts of well-known Bible scriptures on them. Let everyone roam about introducing themselves to each other, and telling their piece of scripture. If you find someone you belong with, stick together until you complete the scripture. For instance, someone with a slip reading, "Even though I walk through the valley of the shadow of death" must find the person with, "I fear no evil, for you are with me," and the other people with the rest of the 23rd Psalm.

This is a good way to divide into discussion groups at a retreat, or just a fun way to get to know each other.

KANGAROO COURT

An effective way to head off hard feelings within your group at a retreat or on a trip is to "prosecute" the culprits in a "kangaroo court."

Three guys in one group splashed three girls while everyone was canoeing on an ice cold lake. The girls didn't see too much humor in their soaked clothes and soggy cameras. Hostile feelings began to brew.

That evening, back at camp, it was announced that a kangaroo court would be held to properly try and prosecute all guilty parties. From that announcement on, everyone began to view the entire incident with a contagious sense of humor.

The defendants were named. A lawyer for the defense was selected, as was a prosecuting attorney. Formal charges were written up and submitted to the judge.

A bailiff and court recorder were appointed. Jurors were screened and sworn in.

By the time the trial began, everyone was laughing so much, they forgot anyone was ever mad.

The trial, complete with witnesses, cross-examinations and outbursts from the defendants, was hilarious.

The three guys were found guilty, but somehow the judge received the penalty—a pie in the face.

A kangaroo court, properly handled, is a great way to settle some group hassles.

CHARIOT RACES

Four people comprise a team. Three of these people grab the front of an old blanket and the other person sits on the end of the blanket. Lay out a race track in any large room and then race around the room. You can have as many teams as the room can hold. Races can be any number of laps around the track.

BUMPER BODS

Everyone squats down and takes hold of his or her own ankles firmly. On the "go" signal, each person tries to bump everyone else over without letting go of his ankles. If anyone is caught with his hands not holding his ankles, he is automatically out. The object of the game is to bump everyone else over while remaining up. There can be only one winner.

This is a great game for outside, but may be played inside also where there is plenty of floor space. It's loads of laughs.

HUMAN CROQUET

Seven of the taller people act as wickets, and position themselves in the regular design for croquet wickets. They spread their legs apart.

The remaining players are divided into two teams, which go to opposite sides of the field or room. One member from each team starts by crawling through the legs of the first wicket, and then each successive wicket, exactly as one plays regular croquet with a mallet and ball. When the first team member has made

it back to the beginning,
the next person on the
team begins. First team
finished is the winner.

LAUGH MACHINE

Have everyone stand in a circle, except someone
who is the laughing machine operator. He stands in the
center. When he raises his hand, he starts the laugh

machine. That means everyone in the circle must laugh at the top of their voices. As soon as the operator brings his hand down, he shuts off the laugh machine. Everyone must stop laughing immediately and keep perfectly silent. If anyone laughs or even lets out a suppressed giggle, he changes places with the person in the center and he starts the laughter machine again.

HOLYWOOD SQUARES

Holywood Squares can be played either as a game or "staged" as a "sermon." As a game it is played as follows, with the questions being biblical or theological:

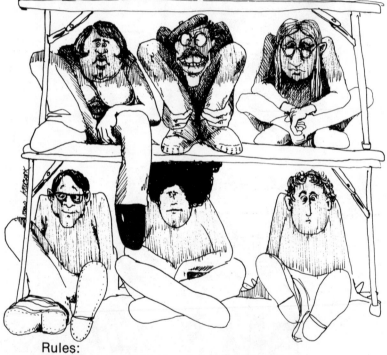

Rules:
1. There are two contestants, one moderator, and nine "square" personalities.
2. Moderator tosses coin to choose starting contestant and assigns the "X" and "O."
3. Starting contestant chooses a square.
4. Moderator asks question of "square" personality.
5. Personality answers correctly or with a bluff.
6. Contestant must agree or disagree in the attempt to obtain the correct answer.

7. If the contestant's choice is correct, the contestant gets the square. If the contestant's choice is incorrect, the opponent gets the square.

8. The game is won when one of the contestants has three of his symbols in a row, horizontally, vertically, or diagonally.

As a sermon it is played in the same manner, however the questions and answers are known ahead of time and coordinated to convey a theme.

FILLING EVERYBODY'S SHOES

Divide the group into two or more teams. Have each team sit in a circle. When a signal to begin is given, each person removes his shoes and passes them to the person on the right. Of course, he also receives a pair of shoes from the person on his left. He must put on the shoes (he doesn't have to take time to tie them) and then remove them again, passing them to the person on his right. This continues all the way around the circle until everyone gets his own shoes back again.

When each person gets his shoes, he has to lace them up and then stand. The first team to have everyone standing wins the prize.

Because of the different sizes of feet, some people will not be able to put on the shoes of other contestants. If anyone gets shoes too small for his feet, he must get his feet in as far as he can, stand, and turn around six times. Because wearing small shoes doesn't help your balance, there will be a lot of laughable tumbles.

COOKIE TOWER

Divide the group into two or more teams. Choose a captain from each team, preferably a person with a balancing ability and the power to restrain from laughing. Each team member is armed with cookies. (Ginger snaps are usually the best, however, "Nilla Wafers" will do in a pinch.) Within a one-minute time limit, the team members must stack as many cookies, one on top of the other, on the captain's forehead. The team with the most cookies stacked wins.

MEASURING FOR A COFFIN

Here's a good "dirty trick" to play on unsuspecting members and/or sponsors.

Instruct your victim to lie on the floor, face up. Tell him you're about to measure him for a coffin. Place a sheet over his entire body, including his face.

Grab his left arm, stretch it out, and measure it with a ruler or tape measure. Call out the length to a record-keeper. Now measure the right arm. Then measure the feet. Now grab a leg, lifting it quite high.

Now for the fun. Unbeknownst to your victim, one of the "morticians" has a glass of ice cold water. As soon as the victim's leg is lifted, the water is dumped down his pant leg. The chilly water will usually run all the way down before the victim leaps to his feet in shock.

FEED YOUR FACE

Divide the group into teams with an equal number of members. If that isn't possible, one of the team members must go twice. Each team will have a paper bag that contains items such as a pea-nut butter and jelly sandwich, a banana, an onion, a lollipop, etc. The bag must contain one item for each person on the team. Team members must not see what is in the bags.

The bags are placed on a shelf a certain distance from each team. On a sig-nal, one member of each team runs up and grabs something from the bag. He must not be able to see what there is to pick. He must eat every single bite of the item before he runs back and tags the next member. The team that is fin-ished first with everything wins.

A. WILKES

PURE CORN

This is a good special event around Halloween or anytime in the fall.

Acquire the use of a large corn field in which the corn has not yet been cut. Cut down several rows to form a maze pattern throughout the field. Have dead ends and surprises along the way. It works best at night. Have a destination point somewhere for everybody to find, where there will be other activities and refreshments. One or two at a time are sent through the maze at different time intervals.

HUFF 'N PUFF COMPETITION

Find a flat surface. . . a table is fine, but the floor will do. Line up facing each other with your chin on the floor or table. Make sure that there are about two inches between ears. You will need two "refs" at the end of the lines.

Place a ping pong ball in the center of the group, and on the signal everyone starts to blow. The object of the game is for one team to blow the ball past the other team.

By the time this has ended, everyone is weak from blowing, laughing and coughing!

BAG IT

This game is really good for learning people's names.

Everybody sits in a circle except for the person who is "IT." "IT" has a paper bag full of air, closed at the open end so the air won't escape. All around the circle, everybody says his name. When that's done, "IT" (from middle of the circle) calls somebody's name and then tries to hit that person over the head with the bag. However, the person whose name was called, calls somebody else's name before he gets hit. Then "IT" has to get that person before he calls another name. It goes like this until "IT" gets somebody or when a name is called when it isn't there. As soon as someone is "got," that person is "IT" and the first "IT" has to say somebody's name before he sits down or can get "got." Then the second "IT" goes until he "gets" someone.

Variations of the game are numerous. Names of countries, states, cities, animals, letters of the alphabet, numbers, bodies of water, signs and symbols. You can also use cartoon characters, or words or books of the Bible, or use your imagination and think up your own.

THIS IS YOUR LIFE

A fun and memorable night can be planned for your youth director or special member by using the old "This Is Your Life" television series idea. This activity works especially well when celebrating a member's or leader's birthday.

"This Is Your Life" requires careful preparation. First, you must learn about the "celebrity's" past without him knowing about your investigating. Find out about important events in his life, and gather a few stories that might be a bit embarrassing to the "celebrity" but funny to the audience.

Arrange for a few old friends, parents, teachers, etc.,

to make surprise appearances at your "This Is Your Life" meeting.

Then, on the big night, have everyone congregate in your auditorium for a "special meeting." Then your selected master of ceremonies will call your surprise "celebrity" to the stage. The emcee then begins telling the story of the "celebrity's" life. As each highlight is reached, a surprise guest walks on from backstage. If you really want to do a professional job, have each surprise guest say a sentence or two into a microphone before appearing on stage.

You can conclude with a party with cake and ice cream for your "celebrity."

"This Is Your Life" may bring a few humble tears to the eyes of your "celebrity," so it's a good idea to have a box of Kleenex handy. This activity is an excellent way for a group to communicate its love for its leader or one of the members.

BANQUET SPEAKERS

This idea is so simple, it's hard to believe it works—till you try it.

The next time your group gets together for a meal, invite "authorities" on various subjects to deliver "banquet speeches." The "authorities" are your group members. Have everyone select a topic on which they wish to deliver a two- or three-minute speech. Or, better yet have one leader assign topics to each speaker just before each is asked to talk.

A kid who just lost his driver's license may be asked to speak on safe driving. A kid who always has messed up hair could speak on today's hair styling. A tall, skinny kid could talk on "How I Solved My Ugly Overweight Problem."

This activity brings out the creativity of each speaker. The results are hilarious.

STATUE-MAKING

Divide your group into pairs. Then, one pair at a time, step to the center of the room. Then, person A makes a "statue" out of person B. Person A puts person B in a position that best indicates how he sees B, or how he sees B's contribution to the group. He places B's arms, legs, etc., in such positions that clearly indicate A's image of B. Props such as chairs may be used if you wish.

Then, B gives his interpretation of A's "creation." After this, A tells if B's interpretation is what he had in mind. If not, A should explain his "statue."

Now B makes a "statue" out of A. This is continued until all have had a turn.

This activity helps to clarify how others see us.

GHOSTS

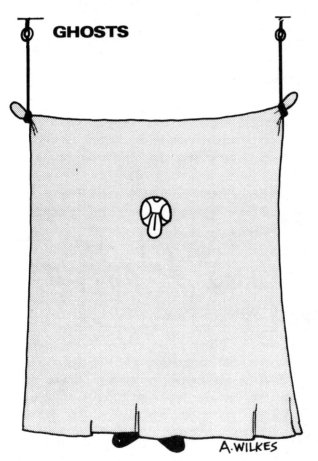

A.WILKES

For this activity you will need a sheet with a small hole near the middle of it. Hang the sheet from the ceiling. Let the group try to identify different people when only the eyes or some feature like the mouth is visible. Make sure the group cannot see the people as they line up behind the sheet. A large box in a doorway may be substituted for the sheet.

DONUT ON A STRING

Have the group pair off—boy and girl teams only! The guys lie on the floor (they should be covered with papers or towels). The girls stand at the boys' feet, armed with a four-foot pole and three feet of string tied on the end of said pole. Tie a donut on the end of the string. The object is to have the guys eat the donut (all of it). However, the problem is that it isn't always easy for the girls to get the donut in the guy's mouth. The guys can't help with their hands. Dunk the donuts in chocolate for extra fun!

MAKE A STAR OF YOUR YOUTH DIRECTOR

This gag takes a little advance planning, but it's one of the funniest ones around.

While eating in a crowded restaurant or waiting in an airport, alert your group members that a "star" is present—your youth director.

Have one of your members near the youth director start to whisper, "Isn't that Jim Smith (or whatever your director's name is) over there?" The kid next to the whisperer affirms it is the "famous" Jim Smith and quietly tells the other kids about the "celebrity" in their presence.

Soon your entire group is gawking and whispering. By this time, other people not with your group should begin to whisper also and start leaning to get a better view of the "star." Some may even say they recognize him from some TV show.

Then, a couple of your members should sheepishly approach the "star" and ask for his autograph.

Soon your entire group surrounds the youth director—all asking for autographs and saying how you've seen one of his movies 27 times.

By this time, if you've done a convincing job, the strangers in the restaurant or airport may also begin to gather around the "star," seeking a closer look and maybe an autograph.

If your youth director isn't in a coma from embarrassment by now, you can escort him to the parking lot, doing your best to fend off the wild-eyed autograph hounds.

PASS THE BODIES

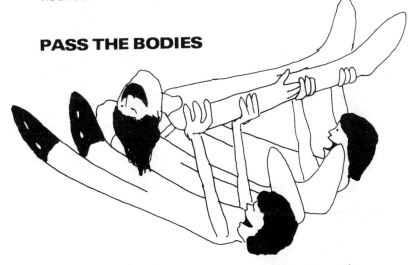

If you have a large group or are at camp, this makes a good game. Divide the group into two teams. Line up each team alternating the feet of one person with the head of another—with everyone lying on their backs on the floor. Select the smallest person on each team. Put him or her at the head of the line. When the signal is given to start, each team passes the person overhead, being careful not to drop him.

NEWSPAPER CRUMPLE

Here's a wild ice breaker. Divide your group into two equal teams. Fasten a rope across the room, about four feet off the floor. Give each team a generous stack of old newspapers.

When signaled to begin, the teams must wad the newspaper and throw it over the rope to the opposing team's territory. The opposing team may then toss it back.

When time is called, usually about three or four minutes, the team with the least amount of wadded newspaper on its side of the room is the winner.

PULLAPART

All of the guys sit on the floor and link arms and legs as tightly as they can. The girls must pull the guys apart. Any tactics are fine. Tickling is okay. In fact, it's one of the best ones. There are no winners, but there is fun, fun, fun!

LEG RALLY

This rally is exactly the same as a car rally, only you walk instead of drive.

Two or three people can go together. Give each group a sheet of questions to answer, such as, "How many cracks are in the sidewalk in front of Zaler's Hardware Store?" The course can be all around the downtown district of the city, or through an area in the country, etc. You always have to walk ahead; if you miss something, you can't go back. Set a time limit. The group with the most answers right wins a prize. To top off the day, go back to the church for a big dinner, fun, games and devotions.

PEOPLE KNOTS

Everyone sits on the floor in a circle with legs extended toward the middle. Each person grabs two others' hands and holds them. The hands cannot be that of either person sitting on your sides and also cannot be the two hands of the same person. Now, everyone stands up and untangles each other into a single circle, without letting go of the hands you have.

It sounds crazy and it is. It's interesting to see people work together and communicate without using their hands.

SIGN-UP MIXER

Find someone to sign their name for each item on the list below. You can ask a person only one question. If the answer is no, you must go to someone else before returning to this person with another question. If the answer is yes, have the person sign your list next to the item. After 10 minutes, the person with the most names will be declared the winner.

——————I use mouthwash regularly
——————I lie about my age
——————I have a hole in my sock right now
——————I have no cavities in my teeth
——————I watch Sesame Street
——————I read Peanuts
——————I was born 1000 miles from here
——————I love Bach
——————I like to play chess
——————I like to read Hemingway
——————I believe in women's lib
——————I cry at movies

_____I eat raw oysters
_____I mash the toothpaste in the middle
_____I dance the Charleston
_____I refuse to walk under a ladder

NAME THAT HYMN

Divide into groups of six to eight each and give each team a distinct noisemaker (cowbell, horn, rattle, etc.). Have someone at the piano begin playing a hymn from your church hymnal or songbook. The team that can identify the title of the hymn makes noise with its noisemaker and identifies the tune. If they're right, they get a point. If wrong, they're penalized one point.

This is a good way to help your group become familiar with the hymn tunes in your hymnal.

GET IN THE NEWS

Get in the news—literally—with a newspaper costume party.

Provide your group with stacks of old newspapers (you'll need plenty), several pairs of scissors, some rolls of Scotch tape, and an abundance of straight pins.

Divide your people into small groups of four or five persons each and make sure each group has the necessary supplies. You'll also need a separate room or corner in which each group can work with privacy (and hilarity).

Each group selects one person to be costumed. After deciding what kind of costume to make, they go to work—cutting, crumpling, bunching, rolling, piecing, pinning, taping.

Allow a certain amount of time (maybe 20 minutes). Then call everybody together for a costume show and awarding of prizes.

FAST ROUND

The entire group sits in a circle with one player sitting in the center. Any small object is passed around the circle while the center player closes his eyes. When the center player says stop, the object stops and the person left holding the object is given any letter of the

alphabet except Q, X, Y or Z by the center player. As the letter is given, the object starts around the circle again.

The person who was caught with the object must name eight objects beginning with the designated letter before the object reaches him again. If he doesn't succeed, he becomes the center person, and the game continues.

The number of objects to be named can be increased or decreased as the game goes on.

THE GOOSE OF SIAM

Have several people leave the room. From those remaining in the room, choose a leader. Bring one person at a time back into the room. The leader tells the person as he enters, that in order to join this group he must bow down before the leader and say, "Owa Tagoo Siam." Have the person say it faster and faster until he realizes he is saying "Oh, what a goose I am." Repeat the procedure as each person is brought back into the room.

COORDINATION

Divide everyone into pairs. Each pair takes a turn, with one partner holding a broom about ten feet away from the the other partner, who throws six jar rings.

The partner holding the broom must keep his foot on the straws, so that the bottom never moves. But he can move the handle as much as possible without moving the bottom to see how many of the jar rings thrown by his partner he can catch on the stick.

After one person throws the rings, the two change places. The six rings are left on the handle and the other person throws six more. The couple with the most rings on the broom wins.

The game can be used strictly as a fun activity, or you can introduce a discussion on cooperation with it, pointing out how difficult it would be to catch any rings at all without both partners working toward a common goal.

SMILE RESISTANCE

See how the members in your group can hold back their laughter.

Have everyone sit in a circle. One person is chosen

to be "IT." He then selects someone in the circle and sits on his or her lap. He then must say, "If ya love me, honey, smile."

Then the person who is being sat upon must say, "I love ya, honey, but I just can't smile." And if he laughs or even smiles, he must become "IT."

The game goes on like this as long as you want. And it usually gets funnier and funnier as it goes along.

REFRIGERAIDER PARTY

Next time your group is looking for something new in the fun-together line, try a "refrigeraider" party. It requires no advance planning, and there are lots of surprises.

Let's say your group is a Sunday school class which decides, on the spur of the moment, to have a party that evening. Ask each member to raid his or her refrigerator before coming and to bring something found there. No fair spending the afternoon at the stove, whipping up something special. The idea of a "refrig-eraider" party is that you bring whatever you already have on hand and share the fun as well as the food.

Possibly you'll end up with an assortment that ranges from leftover potatoes to a carton of milk, from a hunk of cheese to a piece of cake, from meat loaf to mayonnaise. More than likely, you'll be surprised to find that you have all the ingredients of a well-balanced meal. There'll certainly be something for everybody, even if there's not enough of any one thing to go around.

This is a great example of Christian sharing. You offer each other whatever you have, and enjoy the happy glow of fellowship in breaking bread together.

HUMAN CHRISTMAS TREE

Get six volunteers to come to the front. Divide them into two teams. Give each team a box of Christmas decorations. Set a time limit of two minutes.

The team that best decorates one of its members with the ornaments is the winner! The audience should judge which team did the best job.

T-SHIRT TOWER

Place a T-shirt on the floor and see how many people you can get on the shirt without anyone touching the floor. One group's record is 11.

FRISBEE GOLF

Frisbee Golf is a game that can be played outside anywhere.

Each member of the group is asked to bring a Frisbee to the youth gathering or the leader may provide Frisbees for those playing Frisbee Golf. The object of this game is to throw the Frisbee at a designated object and hit it with the least number of throws.

You will need to lay out a course ahead of time by marking the objects to be hit or by giving each player a score card including a map of the course.

The game begins at a starting point where the first group of 4 players will tee off. They individually throw toward the first object. The second throw will be taken from where their first throw landed. Each time they will throw from where their Frisbee lands, until they hit the designated object.

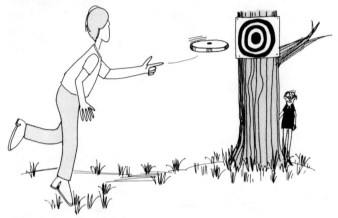

Each person keeps a count of the number of strokes or throws necessary to hit each object along the course.

After the first group has passed the first hole or object, start the next four, and so on until everyone is on the course.

At the completion of the course, the person with the lowest number of strokes or throws is the winner.

You may want to assign a par for your course or give a prize or trophy to your best Frisbee Golfer.

Group Growth Goodies

GETTING TO KNOW YOU

A good way to get to know people in your group is to find out what they like and what they want to become.

Have everyone write on a piece of paper the answers to these questions: What is your favorite food, animal, TV show, hobby, color? Sign your name. Don't let anyone else see your answers. Give the answer sheets to the leader. The leader then reads the answers to the whole group. And members try to guess whom each set of answers belongs to.

Award one point for each right guess. The person with the most points wins a prize.

A LABEL ON YOUR FOREHEAD

Here's a fun game that both makes a great ice breaker and offers insight and empathy to others' feelings.

Cut strips of paper about one inch wide and six inches long. Place a three-foot-long length of string or yarn on each strip, taping the string to the paper. On the other side of the paper, write the names of various types of personalities: "introvert," "extrovert," "shy," "obnoxious," "lonely," "sad," "caring," etc.

Then, tie the strings around each kid's head with the label showing on his forehead. Make sure no one sees his label as it is put on.

Now, have everyone mill around in the room, conversing with one another. No one may tell another what his label is. But each person is to be treated as you would treat a person with the characteristic listed on his forehead.

After the "milling around" period is over, everyone gets to remove his label and see it. Then discuss how you felt about the way you were treated, and how long it took you to discover "who you are." Also, think about how you treated the various other labeled people.

There are many variations to this game. Try this group of labels: "preacher," "Jesus freak," "atheist," "Jew," "Christian," "agnostic," etc. Or this group: "old woman," "little sister," "rich uncle," "mother," "father," "grandfather," etc.

It's okay to give the same name to more than one kid. Sometimes it's interesting to see how two "lonely" labeled people, for instance, may find each other in the "milling around" period and enjoy each others' company.

LOVE SERVICE

This is what you call a "love service" and can be done with large and small groups.

Proceed as follows: seat everyone in a circle and the leader should have a lighted candle and stand in the center of the circle. The lights should be out. The leader is to think of someone in the group and, without mentioning his name, tell why he loves this person in the love Christ gave him. After he has finished this he hands the candle to the one he's talking about and that person repeats the procedure.

The candle is meant as a token of love. The meeting should last until everyone has at least one turn.

This is an experience in love that will not easily be forgotten. Participants should not be afraid of sharing emotions.

ROVING PHOTO SCREENS

A very pleasing effect for your next worship service or multi-media program is quite easy to perform.

Construct one or more screens-on-a-stick. A large piece of white cardboard tacked to a long stick will do.

Now project your slides or movies onto the screens held by the group members. The screens can be moved about to create very interesting effects.

The projector can be left stationary while the screen moves to the left and right and up and down—catching the projected image as it passes. The screen can also be moved closer to the projector—"zooming in" on one portion of the image. Or, the projectionist can follow the screen as it moves.

You can achieve a dazzling effect by using several projectors and several screens, all roving about the room catching images everywhere.

TINKERTOY COMMUNICATION

This exercise illustrates the importance of face-to-face, verbal communication.

Before your group meets, your leader should build a Tinkertoy structure using 20 to 25 pieces. Make sure no one sees it.

Divide the group into teams of six people. Provide each group with Tinkertoys identical to those used by the leader. Each group chooses a captain, whose job it is to look at the leader's structure and then send messages to his team on how to build an identical structure. The captain may not draw it; he may only describe it. Each team may send questions back to their captain at any time. You will need runners to take messages back and forth.

The winner is determined both by speed and resemblance to the original structure.

SONG SIGNS

Teaching your congregation a new song for Youth Sunday? Tired of seeing the people bury their faces, and voices, in the songbook? Here's an idea to get them to look, and sing, forward.

Letter the lyrics on large pieces of posterboard. Give one poster to each kid standing in front of the congregation. As the song progresses, each poster is held up for the congregation to see and read.

It's kind of like the old "follow the bouncing ball" routine.

This method works especially well with simple songs with few lyrics, such as "Day by Day."

YARN CIRCLE

Unity and cooperation are vital ingredients in any successful group. These qualities can be graphically demonstrated in a "yarn circle."

Everyone should stand in a circle. Someone begins by mentioning something he is thankful for. He then tosses a ball of yarn to another person in the circle, being careful to hang on to the end of the yarn. The recipient of the ball of yarn then mentions something he's thankful for, and tosses it to another person, holding on to his bit of yarn. This goes on until everyone has had a chance to contribute at least once. By this time, the yarn should have created an intricate pattern, interweaving all of your members.

Then, slowly, a few of the members should drop their sections of yarn, making the pattern sag. In order to take up the slack, all remaining members of the circle must back up. Repeat this a couple of times.

Then, everyone should have a chance to reflect on what just occurred. It should be brought out that the beautiful pattern was possible only with everyone's involvement. And when some members dropped out of the involvement, the yarn design became ugly and the group was ultimately forced to grow farther apart.

This is a good exercise to repeat periodically.

SPONSOR A KID

Your group can be responsible for sending a disadvantaged kid to school, or feeding a hungry kid, or providing medical care to a needy child.

All you need to do is commit yourselves to bringing a set amount of money to each meeting. If you have 20 members and each brings just 25 cents per week, in a month you'll have $20. That's usually enough to provide the necessary services for a needy child overseas.

Have one of your members in charge of collecting the money each week and sending it off at the end of the month.

Some of the organizations that can set you up in sponsoring a kid are: World Vision International, 919 W. Huntington Drive, Monrovia, CA 91016; Food for the Hungry, Inc., Box E, Scottsdale, AZ 85252; Christian Children's Fund, Inc., Box 26511, Richmond, VA 23261; Compassion, Inc., Box 7000, Colorado Springs, CO 80933.

With a bit of commitment and prayer your group can make a significant impact in our troubled world.

KID-PARENT ROLE REVERSAL

You can have great fun with a role play situation with kids and parents in your church.

Prepare questions concerning dating, morals, current events, etc. Youth answer "as if" they're parents. Parents answer "as if" they're teenagers.

Some sample questions:

1. How old should you be to date?
2. What time should you be home?
3. Should a 10th grade girl double date?
4. Should you date on week nights?
5. Should you make your child go to Sunday school?
6. What do you do on a date besides "park"?
7. How do you feel about teenage drinking?
8. What should you do if you feel your child has the "wrong" friends?
9. How much money should you give your child?
10. How do you resolve a conflict with your parents?

The leader must make sure that each person speaking stays in his or her role.

MULTIPLYING MONEY

Here's an experience based on Matthew 25:14-29. This is the story of the three servants who were given sums of money by their master. The master left on a trip. When he returned, two of the servants reported they had invested the money and multiplied it for their master. But the third servant had buried the money he had been given. This servant told his master that he was afraid the master would rob him of the profit he earned, so he hid the money until the master's return. The master was angry and told the servant he could have at least put the money in the bank where it would have earned interest.

At one church, instead of the offering being collected one Sunday, the plate was passed around full of dollar bills with the invitation to take one. More than 300 dollar bills were taken, and were put to work by members of the congregation. They gathered in the church parking lot one Sunday to sell items they had made and grown.

Many types of goods were sold. There were macrame owls, wall hangings, pot hangers, edible painted pies, homemade bread, plaques, paintings, jewelry, flowers, homemade noodles and fresh garden vegetables. Also personal services were provided, such as babysitting, window washing and lawn care.

The proceeds gathered went to feed the hungry of the world.

This same idea would work just as well with just the youth group. The $1 is bound to grow unless it's buried in the ground.

TRIP JOURNAL

Going on a trip this summer? You will probably experience some of the best times of your life on the trip. These times will be too good to forget. So, get a volunteer or two from the group to write a trip journal.

At the end of each day of your trip, the journal writer should sit down and write out everything that happened that day. Include good and bad things, laughs and miseries, fun and boring times. Be sure to include lots of the kids' names. Matter of fact, it's best if you can mention each member for each day of the trip.

Write the journal like a diary—a separate entry for each day. Don't let anyone else see your journal entries.

When you return from the trip, type out the journal and have it mimeographed. You may want to add some artwork on the cover, or a map showing the trail of your journey.

Then, set aside a part of one of your regular meetings to pass out the journals. Everybody will look forward to them with as much (or more) anticipation than your school yearbooks.

Your trip journal will become one of your prized possessions, read and re-read year after year.

ME METER

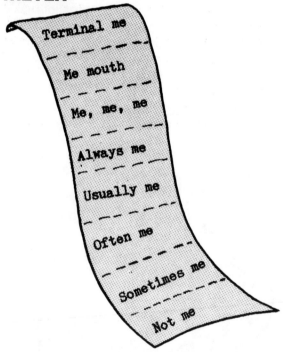

Plan an entire meeting where everybody is forbidden to say "I," "me," "myself" or any other reference to self.

At the beginning of the meeting, each member is given a mimeographed paper strip, like the one above. This Me Meter should be pinned on the front of each person. Then proceed with your meeting—mixer, discussion, refreshments, etc. Each time a member refers to himself, the nearest person to him tears off the bottom section of the self-violator's Me Meter.

A cheap hand mirror should be awarded to the member who has the shortest Me Meter at the end of the meeting. The message "My Favorite Subject" should be written with Magic Marker on the face of the mirror.

The very experience of trying to speak without mentioning yourself is very eye-opening and thought-provoking. You may think twice the next time you're tempted to talk about yourself or offer your own criticism, opinion or complaint to a situation that would benefit from your silence.

You may want to reserve a period of time at the end of the meeting for a discussion of how we often dominate our speech with references to ourselves.

For really brave and ambitious groups, plan an entire weekend retreat where "I" and "me" are forbidden.

ROSTER

One of the most effective tools in a youth group is also one of the simplest—a roster.

Obtain each member's name, address, and phone number, and mimeograph the list. The size of your group makes no difference. This roster will be highly used by leaders and members alike. Make sure everyone has a copy.

When you need to notify everybody for a special meeting or activity, use the roster as a "pass it on" telephone list. Have your leader call the first kid on the list with the message. That kid calls the next kid, and so on. If the kid below your name is not home, you should call the following name—then, at a later time, call the name below yours again. In this way, your group message won't get hung up somewhere. You may want to print the "pass it on" instructions right at the top of the roster.

Also, the roster works well for "chain letter" communication. For a special group event, the first kid on the list sends a personal letter to the next person— with instructions that the letter must be sent to the next person, or the chain will be broken. Each person adds a personal note to the letter and sends it on to the next kid. You should include a roster in the mailing in case one of your members has lost his copy. The "chain letter" should be started well in advance of the event you're promoting.

Everybody likes mail and phone calls from friends, so these two uses of your roster are sure winners.

The roster and its uses also tend to re-excite kids who may have drifted away from your group. They're kept posted of your activities, and there's a good chance they'll return.

Update your roster often, adding the names of new members and making address corrections, etc. And make sure everyone gets a copy every time you update.

SYMBOLIC GIFTS

Divide your group into subgroups of about eight persons. Then each of the eight should hunt around the church, home, or wherever you're meeting, for seven items that would make symbolic gifts of love to the other people in the group.

Allow plenty of time for the hunt, perhaps as much as an hour. Careful thought should be given to the selection of each gift.

Examples: You might find some paper and cut it into little bits, making confetti. This might represent joy for a person in your group who needs some cheering up. Or, you might find a telephone book, symbolizing your appreciation to a person in the group who has phoned you when you were lonely.

After everyone has gathered all the gifts he intends to give, re-group and sit in a circle. Then, one at a time, each member receives his gifts from the seven other members. An explanation of each gift should be made as you give it to the recipient.

This is a sharing of love. Jokes and gag gifts should be avoided.

These gifts just could be the most beautiful you'll receive this Christmas.

SECRET BIBLE STUDY

After discussing the hardships of Christians in Communist nations one Sunday, one group decided to have a Bible study that characterized a meeting behind the Iron Curtain.

No one parked near the home in which the meeting was held. There were no lights on in the house (candles were the only light). They arranged to have the meeting interrupted by policemen who pulled up to the house with lights flashing, pounded on the door, and confiscated all the Bibles (this was a surprise to the kids). They then went around the room and shared verses of scripture that they had memorized. They finished the meeting by observing the Lord's Supper.

It made everyone more thankful for our freedom to worship, and more mindful of the persecutions of Christians in other countries.

DIFFERENT INGREDIENTS

This activity will provide your entertainment, Bible study, discussion, and refreshment if your group has access to a kitchen.

You will need two cooks, a cake recipe and the ingredients. One cook should have the correct ingredients and the other one should have different incorrect ingredients. He or she should substitute lard for butter and rock salt for sugar. The lousy cook can also be missing some ingredients and use the wrong measurements. . . anything to add humor to the situation. It's a good idea to have the bad cook with a clear bowl and the good cook with a non-transparent bowl.

The good cook tells how to make the cake and occasionally glances over to see how the bad cook is doing.

Finally, when they are done with the mixing, they both place the ingredients in pans. The good cook places his/her ingredients in a cake pan, and the bad cook places his/her ingredients on a cookie sheet.

Then the cakes are placed in the oven to bake while your group discusses how different ingredients in a person's life can make a person what he is. What does the ingredient of Christ do to a person's life?

When the cakes are finished, you can compare them, and, of course, eat the better one.

The ingredients for your good cake can come straight from the Bible. Here is the recipe:

4½ cups 1 Kings 4:22
1 cup Judges 5:25 (last clause)
2 cups Jeremiah 6:20
2 cups 1 Samuel 30:12
2 cups Nahum 3:12
2 cups Numbers 17:8
6 Jeremiah 17:11
½ cup Judges 4:19 (last clause)
2 tbsp. 1 Samuel 14:25
Pinch or more of Leviticus 2:13
Season to taste with 2 Chronicles 9:9
2 tsp. Amos 4:5

A GIFT OF LOVE

A Christmas Gift of Love need not be limited to the yuletide calendar. It is useful throughout the year in helping us look at the way we give gifts. After all, the spirit of Christmas, even beyond its particular religious significance, often truly means giving and sharing and getting in return. These are not necessarily material gifts, but giving the gift of oneself and experiencing the love of friends.

Take a piece of paper and divide it into four columns from top to bottom. In the first, list the five friends who are closest to you. Then list three to five members of your family who are very close to you. In the second column, list the gifts you gave to those people last Christmas. These should be actual material gifts.

In the third column, list a gift of the Spirit that you might give to each of these people. This gift would be a special quality, such as love, kindness, patience, or humor, that would most help that particular person in his quest for a better life. Give each of these eight to ten people a carefully chosen intangible gift that you believe would make that person happier.

In the fourth column, list the gift that each of these people might give you, something you think they might feel you need based on their close knowledge of you. What quality would each of these people like to see you have? Maybe their gifts of behavorial or personality change would be similar. If so, it might tell you something useful about yourself, your friends, and your relationships with them.

You can help other people achieve their goals by giving them what you think they would want, but most importantly, you can help them achieve their goals by giving them the year-round gift of love: friendship. In a sense, that is the ultimate value.

CHRISTMAS CARD DELIVERY

Since postage is becoming so expensive and people no longer send many Christmas cards, one youth group decided to deliver Christmas cards for its congregation free of charge. This is an outline of how they did it:

"1. Set up boundaries of the delivery area. Make the church the center of your map. Since we live in Philadelphia, we chose approximately one mile in each direction as the boundary for our delivery. Perhaps if in a rural area, you could cover more area.

"2. Notify the congregation of your plan. Give the congregation two weeks notice as to when the deliveries will be made so they can have their cards in on time. Ask them to put their return address on the envelope in case of a questionable address on the envelope. Make sure the congregation knows the boundaries. A good way to do this would be to draw a map showing the boundaries. Set at least two delivery dates in case you are inundated with mail. We chose the two Sundays before Christmas and delivered cards all afternoon.

"3. Decorate a big box into which the cards can be placed. Put the box in a convenient location where all can see it.

"4. Divide the cards up according to city blocks or districts, whatever is suitable to your surroundings. Cards placed in the box that do not fit into the specified boundaries should be returned to the sender. Divide your group up into four smaller groups to cover north, south, east, and west districts around the church. Send each district out in appropriate number of cars. Make one person in each car in charge of seeing that all of their mail is delivered. Delivery must take place in a quiet, orderly manner because this is a witness to the neighborhood. Meet back at the church to make sure everyone finished safely.

"5. Show gratitude to the workers (optional). Our congregation thought this was such a great and unique idea that when we returned both Sunday afternoons the women of our church prepared a huge smorgasbord dinner for us. Some people donated the money they saved in stamps to our youth group.

"Both days we delivered cards we ran into terrible weather. The first day we had torrential rains and the second day it snowed. This can be extremely hazardous. Our group had a lot of fun in this endeavor. It was a lot of work for us—we delivered over 1,500 cards in only two afternoons. The congregation was very appreciative."

TREE SANTAS

You can bring a lot of joy to disadvantaged families in your area this Christmas with very little expense.

Visit the Christmas tree lots in your area and see if the owners will agree to let your group have all their leftover trees on Christmas Eve or before.

Obtain from a local social service office, or perhaps your church, a list of all those families in your area that cannot afford a Christmas tree.

Then, when you get your truckload of trees, get together and deliver a Christmas tree to each of the needy families. They'll really be surprised—and grateful.

TRICK-OR-TREAT REVERSED

The kids in your group have probably profited a good deal from the people in your congregation and neighborhood. They've probably carted away a couple truckloads of trick-or-treat candy.

Here's an idea your group can use to return some of that goodness back to your neighborhood. When you go Christmas caroling, take along sacks of Christmas candies and cookies. After you've sung your song on the doorstep, give the people inside a sack of goodies. This is a fine act of love and Christmas giving.

You can have a lot of fun getting together before your caroling party, too, baking and decorating the cookies and candies.

FAVORING THE OLD FOLKS

Halloween can be a very special event for old people. A number of good activities can be planned at a local rest home for the enjoyment of the residents.

Don't be afraid to consider organizing a costume party for the oldsters. They may surprise you with their originality and enthusiasm.

Also, some of the old-timers often have some dandy spook stories to tell around a dim candle.

Fun Fund Raisers

BUY THE BEARD

This one takes very little effort, and it's 100 per-cent profit.

All you need to do is ask your youth sponsor to grow a beard, then sit back and let the comments roll in. Then simply begin two collections to allow people to voice their opinions as to the "morality" of a youth minister growing a beard.

The kids in one group collected the money during the coffee hour. They wore signs on their backs so people would know to which side they were giving the money. These signs said "Shave It Off" or "Keep It On." If you are lucky, someone will voice the idea that they will "make up the difference, just to ensure that the youth sponsor will shave." Once word of that gets around, people start supporting the "Keep It On" side knowing that their money will be doubled.

SPOOK INSURANCE

A piece of the Pumpkin

**THE JACK O. LANTERN
INSURANCE COMPANY**
OFFICIAL POLICY

Last Halloween, did your neighbors and friends have trouble with ghosties and goblins? Did they wake up in the morning to find their windows soaped, their yards covered with trash, rotten tomatoes on their cars?

This year, why doesn't your youth group protect these unfortunate people and earn some money at the same time?

"The Jack O. Lantern Insurance Company" will sell "a piece of the pumpkin" to individuals who want to insure their dwelling, automobile, property, or all three. Prices vary according to the type of policy.

"Jack O. Lantern" policies guarantee that your group will clean any damages caused as a result of "spooks" on Halloween night, provided they are reported by the specified date.

Here's how one group set up its policies:

Coverage A. . . . dwelling. . . . 75¢
Coverage B. . . . automobile. . . . 75¢
Coverage C. . . . property. . . . 75¢
Coverage D. . . . all perils. . . . $2
This coverage includes any act in which the following are used: eggs, soap, tomatoes, watermelons, shaving cream, marshmallow cream, toilet paper, or trash.

This coverage does not include and specifically disallows vandalism and malicious mischief, meaning only the willful and malicious damage to, or destruction of, the property covered. [Examples would be burning, painting, broken windows, etc.]

Claims must be reported by November 2, before 6 p.m.

All cleaning or clearing will be done midnight, November 2.

To report claims, call one of the following phone numbers.

Start with your congregation, and make sure everybody is offered a policy. Then, each of your members should go door to door in his or her neighborhood selling policies.

Your mimeographed policy should have spaces for the insured's name and address and the type of policy desired. Use a carbon, making a copy for the insured and for your group.

Then, have teams of two or three kids that can be dispatched to the houses reporting "attacks" from Halloween tricksters.

This is a fun fund-raiser, and your only expenses are the mimeographed policy flyers and a couple bottles of cleanser. Plus, you're providing a very useful service!

WRAP-UP FUND RAISER

Looking for a good wintertime fund raiser? Try wrapping presents. Talk to the manager of a large department store, shopping center or shopping mall and get his permission to set up a wrapping booth. Then, charge shoppers to wrap their purchases, while they wait.

You'll need a selection of wrapping paper, ribbon and bows. And you should have some empty boxes on hand for items that come to you unboxed.

Put wrapped sample boxes on display with price tags. You'll probably want to set different prices for wrapping small, medium and large boxes. Then, when a customer comes with a box to be wrapped, you must determine which sample size most closely matches the customer's, and charge accordingly.

Determine your costs for wrapping, ribbon and bow, and then double or triple that, and you should come up with a fair price. Charge extra if you have to furnish the box. And you may wish to offer a fancier wrapping paper for a greater price.

Gifts Wrapped Here

Be sure to post a sign that shows your group's name and possibly the reason you're raising the money.

Try to persuade a store owner to sell you the wrapping paper and bows at a discount.

Before you get started, invite one of the moms to teach all your members how to wrap a present professionally.

And, be sure to have your booth well staffed so shoppers do not have to wait a long time for your service.

Note

Every youth group knows some good ideas for worships, games, crowd breakers, discussions, activities or fund raisers. We urge you to share those successful ideas with others. GROUP Magazine is always looking for ideas that really work in youth groups, and we'll pay you for each one we use.

Mail ideas to:

"Try This One"
GROUP
P.O. Box 481
Loveland, CO 80539

OTHER YOUTH MINISTRY RESOURCES FROM

DENNIS BENSON'S CREATIVE BIBLE STUDIES, BY DENNIS C. BENSON. This huge resource offers 401 complete, creative Bible studies for ALL of Matthew, Mark, Luke, John and Acts. 660 pages. $19.95.

COUNSELING TEENAGERS, BY DR. G. KEITH OLSON. The authoritative, complete, and practical reference for understanding and helping today's adolescents. Hardbound, 528 pages. $19.95.

THE YOUTH WORKER'S PERSONAL MANAGEMENT HANDBOOK. Provides unique help for youth workers as they seek to better control and manage their professional and personal lives. Hardbound. $16.95.

THE BASIC ENCYCLOPEDIA FOR YOUTH MINISTRY, BY DENNIS BENSON & BILL WOLFE. Answers, ideas, encouragement, and inspiration for 230 youth ministry questions and problems. A handy reference. Hardbound. $15.95.

THE GROUP RETREAT BOOK, BY ARLO REICHTER. This is the resource for start-to-finish retreat planning, execution and evaluation . . . plus 34 ready-to-use retreat outlines. 400 pages. $15.95.

HARD TIMES CATALOG FOR YOUTH MINISTRY, BY MARILYN & DENNIS BENSON. Hundreds of low-cost and no-cost ideas for programs, projects, meetings and activities. $14.95.

THE YOUTH GROUP HOW-TO BOOK. Detailed instructions and models for 66 practical projects and programs to help you build a better group. $14.95.

SPIRITUAL GROWTH IN YOUTH MINISTRY, BY J. DAVID STONE. Offers help for youth workers to grow in their relationship with God. Also offers incredible opportunities for spiritual growth in youth groups. Hardbound. $12.95.

CREATIVE WORSHIP IN YOUTH MINISTRY, BY DENNIS C. BENSON. An ideas-packed resource for youth worship in various settings—Youth Sundays, youth group meetings, retreats and camps, many more. $11.95.

THE YOUTH GROUP MEETING GUIDE, BY RICHARD W. BIMLER. This resource provides years of inspiration, ideas and programs for the most common youth group activity—the meeting. $11.95.

BUILDING COMMUNITY IN YOUTH GROUPS, BY DENNY RYDBERG. Offers practical guidance and workable ideas to develop a caring Christian youth group. Over 100 creative activities. $11.95.

CLOWN MINISTRY, BY FLOYD SHAFFER & PENNE SEWALL. Everything you need to know to begin a clown ministry or enhance your present ministry. Includes 30 detailed skits and more than 50 short clowning ideas. $7.95.

VOLUNTEER YOUTH WORKERS, BY J. DAVID STONE & ROSE MARY MILLER. A step-by-step process for involving adults in a vital youth ministries program. $6.95.

STARTING A YOUTH MINISTRY, BY LARRY KEEFAUVER. An insightful book with tips on starting a youth ministry program or revitalizing an existing program. $5.95.

THE BEST OF TRY THIS ONE (Volume 1). A fun collection of games, crowdbreakers and programs from GROUP Magazine's "Try This One" section. $5.95.

MORE . . . TRY THIS ONE (Volume 2). A bonanza of youth group ideas— crowdbreakers, stunts, games, discussions and fund raisers. $5.95.

TRY THIS ONE . . . TOO (Volume 3). Scores of creative youth ministry ideas. $5.95.

TRY THIS ONE . . . STRIKES AGAIN (Volume 4). The newest in this popular series. A gold mine of original, simple and fun youth group activities. $5.95.

FRIEND TO FRIEND, BY J. DAVID STONE & LARRY KEEFAUVER. Provides a simple yet powerful method for helping a friend sort through thoughts, feelings and behaviors of life problems. $4.95.

PEW PEEVES. A humorous look at all those little things that drive you crazy in church. $3.95.

Available at Christian bookstores or directly from the publisher: Group Books, Box 481, Loveland, CO 80539. Enclose $2 for postage and handling with each order from the publisher.